the forgotten horses

the forgotten horses

PHOTOGRAPHS BY Tony Stromberg

FOREWORD BY Robert Redford

New World Library
Novato, California

New World Library
14 Pamaron Way
Novato, California 94949

Design by Mary Ann Casler

Library of Congress Cataloging-in-Publication Data
Stromberg, Tony.
The forgotten horses / photographs by Tony Stromberg ;
foreword by Robert Redford.
      p.   cm.
ISBN 978-1-57731-615-2 (hardcover : alk. paper)
1. Horses--Pictorial works. 2. Horses--Anecdotes.
3. Photography of horses. I. Title.
SF303.S826 2008
636.1´0832--dc22   2008007026

First printing, September 2008
ISBN 978-1-57731-615-2
Printed in China

10 9 8 7 6 5 4 3 2 1

To unwanted horses, both domestic and wild

To the unsung heroes at equine rescue organizations and sanctuaries all over the world who have taken it upon themselves to honor, defend, care for, and support unwanted horses and animals — it is their life, their livelihood, and their homecoming

foreword

HORSES HAVE ALWAYS SPOKEN TO ME on a deep and personal level. They are an elemental bridge between the ancient rhythms of nature and the contemporary human being.

But what really drew me to write the foreword to this book were the beautiful images. Tony Stromberg's remarkable photographs express the beauty, grace, spirit, and devotion that all horses embody — their sometimes invisible essence.

Over the years, the horse has been misunderstood in many ways, and those misconceptions continue to be perpetuated. In Western mythology, horses have sometimes been subordinated (although affectionately so), as with such fictional characters as Trigger, Flicka, Silver, and National Velvet. In real life, they have been maligned as objects to be kicked, whipped, spurred, and beaten into submission — treated as wild beasts to be conquered and tamed by man's superiority.

What's missing, of course, is the larger, finer picture of who and what these animals really are. Those who have spent time with horses — particularly those without the burden of training them for utilitarian purposes — know the deeper spirit of this animal. This is especially true for those who have had the honor of knowing a horse from birth, of knowing it as a companion.

As for my own personal philosophy about horses, I will let my work with them in films like *The Electric Horseman* and *The Horse Whisperer* speak for itself, as the characters I portrayed in these films honestly reflect my feelings.

As for this book, Tony Stromberg's photographs capture the special essence of the horse; many have tried to capture that archetypal spirit in photographs, but very few have succeeded.

Robert Redford,
April 2008

introduction

I STARTED THIS BOOK WITH NO IDEA HOW IT WOULD TURN OUT. I simply wanted to continue doing what I love: photographing horses and spending time with them. I had thought that publishing my previous book, *Spirit Horses*, was one of those major life accomplishments that would allow me to coast for a while. I did not realize that, in my early fifties, I was just beginning my life's true work. I now know that *Spirit Horses*, and this book, are steps on an ever-unfolding pilgrimage toward freedom for me.

A book like this can, and probably must, take on a life of its own. *The Forgotten Horses* certainly has. I feel like its midwife as much as its author or photographer, as I have watched it unfold from within and blossom. Once again, I have learned that it is usually best to simply clear my mind of preconceptions or agendas, get out of the way, and let what wants to happen simply happen. I realize that I have become, in some inexplicable way, a conduit for the voice of a very magnificent form of life. And I am deeply honored to help make that voice heard.

When I published *Spirit Horses*, I began to receive emails and letters from people telling me how much the book meant to them. Many of those people were not horse owners or horse aficionados. Rather, they worked in office buildings all day, on the phone or in front of computers. Many of them were not all that happy and felt a distinct lack of meaning in their lives. The following excerpt, from a letter sent to me by a woman named Maria, exemplifies the hundreds I've received:

> *I would just like to let you know that your work has made quite an impact and impression on me emotionally....With every passing day my yearning to leave civilization and live closer to nature and horses gets stronger and stronger. I admire the move you made. Thank you for giving the world an opportunity to see the true spirit of the horse.*

No matter where they were from or what they did for a living, those who wrote to me all shared the same underlying longing, the same quiet tone of restlessness, and the same desire to reconnect with something lost. These letters made me think more deeply about why horses speak to people so strongly, even people who have never been around them in person. Horses

seem to be archetypal messengers, their essence somehow bridging the gap between the earth and that greater realm where we are all ultimately bound. They also embody qualities that many of us would like to bring back into our lives — qualities we have forgotten or given away — freedom, power, and integrity the foremost among them.

I don't know when it all changed for me. But I remember feeling increasingly uncomfortable every time I drove by fenced-in horses. What once seemed completely normal somehow didn't anymore. And these feelings stuck with me and forced me into deeper and deeper layers of personal inquiry. I started to realize that these feelings might reflect the journey my own life has taken since I left my job as a big-city commercial photographer and pursued a simpler life photographing horses. The more I freed myself from containment and structure, the more I found myself awakening to imprisonment in the world around me. The more I *chose* what to do with my life, and where and how to do it, the more aware I became of why I had felt so trapped in my old life. Like most people, I had done things the way I was supposed to rather than following a deeper inspiration. And the more I sought liberation, the more I noticed everyone else longing for the same liberation.

I thought about how we live in our technologically driven culture and about what we truly value; eventually I came to wonder whether we even know what we truly value. I read recently that only about 5 percent of the U.S. population lives in a rural environment, in contrast to the 25 to 30

percent of us who lived there fifty years ago. We have made a huge migration toward urban life. As a consequence, we are that much farther removed from the natural world around us.

And then this epiphany suddenly dawned on me: *we do to our animals what we do to ourselves.* We assume they have no problem leading lives that mirror those we have created for ourselves — structured and contained, sterile and controlled, with increasingly small doses of true freedom and playful abandon.

Our urbanized lives have created an increasing hunger for connection to the wilderness. Yet we don't recognize this hunger for what it is. Instead, we try to satiate it with entertainment, devices, appliances, clothes — *things* that hold momentary fascination and provide fleeting satisfaction. But then there we are again, craving the latest gizmo to replace the last gizmo that doesn't feel as fast or fancy anymore.

We have become a society whose mantra is disposability. In our misdirected quest for some elusive sense of perfection, we act like hungry ghosts, caught in an endless cycle of consumption. We tire quickly of our cars, our toys, our tools, our clothes — and nowadays even our animals and our loved ones — but no matter, we can simply toss them aside and replace them. The horses we have tossed aside are the subject of this book.

Nobody is to blame. We just forgot. We forgot the value the natural world can bring us. We are like abusive parents passing down what they

themselves were taught. We have simply lost touch with what gives us peace and belonging, the feeling that we have enough and are an integral part of the world around us.

In the introduction to his beautiful little book *Kinship with All Life*, J. Allen Boone prophetically writes:

> *Men and women everywhere are being made acutely aware of the fact that something essential to life and well-being is flickering very low in the human species and threatening to go out entirely. This "something" has to do with such values as love . . . sincerity . . . loyalty . . . honesty . . . enthusiasm . . . humility . . . goodness . . . happiness . . fun. Practically every animal still has these assets in abundance and is eager to share them, given opportunity and encouragement.*

Horses, and all animals, can bring to our lives a true gift — not just ribbons, trophies, or dollars. Through a marvelous cocreative process, horses are trying to show us a way back to a place they have never left.

MY VISION FOR THIS BOOK BEGAN TO CRYSTALLIZE when I started to notice that some of the horses I've had the pleasure to meet in the past, including some featured in my first book, were simply not around anymore. When I started investigating, I found that many of them had been "put down" (a euphemism for killed) because they had become lame, had fallen short of being championship material, had a deformity, or hadn't been able to breed or carry foals anymore, thereby becoming unprofitable.

Around the same time, I started visiting horse shelters, sanctuaries, and rescue organizations while scouting new locations for my photography workshops. In the process, I met some unique and remarkable horses and began to photograph them for this book. My original plan was to tell each of those horses' unique stories. Sadly, I came to learn that many of the stories were not so unique — their tragedies were so remarkably similar that they did not bear repeating. It also became apparent that in some cases no one knew their stories.

Many of these horses had been unloaded at livestock auctions, which frequently lead to the slaughterhouse. Agents buy up horses at auction and then sell them directly to slaughterhouses, which pay for horses by the pound. Much of the money people donate to rescue organizations and sanctuaries is used to outbid these agents. Although the recent court-mandated closure of American slaughterhouses was a welcome victory for horses, the lack of federal protection at our borders means that horses are now being shipped to Mexico or Canada, where their deaths are rendered even more cruelly.

Another common story is that of the rescued PMU mare. PMU stands for Pregnant Mare Urine, which is what the brand-name pharmaceutical Premarin is named for. Developed and marketed as a hormone replacement therapy for women, the primary ingredient in the drug comes from the urine of pregnant mares. The mares are tied all day long wearing bags to collect

their urine. After they give birth, they spend the summer at pasture with their foals, an unwanted by-product of this industry, before starting another cycle. Each year around thirty thousand foals are born, although this number is dropping quickly as new research shows that Premarin is causing cancer in women. PMU mares have historically been very large draft horses, the kind used to plow fields and pull heavy wagons. Draft horses have the patience to stand tied all day, and they are so large that their foals typically weigh one thousand pounds at one year and so bring a good price at auction. PMU foals are weaned in the fall and then sold at auction to the meat market, and the meat is typically sold overseas, where it is considered a delicacy. The decline of the PMU industry is both a blessing and a temporary curse — a blessing in that a very inhumane industry is quickly disappearing, and a curse because thousands of draft horse mares and foals suddenly need homes.

Many of the horses who find their way directly to local horse shelters also share common stories. Some are horses who cannot be ridden competitively for one reason or another. Others are the horses of children who have grown up and moved on to college. Many are the results of experiments in cross-breeding that did not work out as hoped. Others were simply abandoned, usually because of financial hardship — left in a field or lot to slowly starve until someone notices them and calls the sheriff. I even heard about one pair of horses abandoned inside a closed wooden barn, forced by starvation to literally eat their way out. One survived; his companion did not.

An inordinate number of horses fall victim to a common pattern — one you hear about again and again around the stable. Someone buys a horse for pleasure and everything goes well until an unexpected behavioral issue arises. These issues often result from the old methods of training, which are often based on control and punishment, rather than true partnership. The issue gets worse, and the owner doesn't know how to deal with the problematic horse. Ultimately, after trying a few different trainers, he or she ends up selling the horse, either privately or through a local auction.

The reasons horses are disposed of are almost endless: I learned about ex-racehorses who had earned their owners hundreds of thousands of dollars, only to be disposed of just days after an injury precluded their competing anymore. I heard about one horse left as collateral at a convenience store while the owner went to get money to pay for gas and sodas; he never returned. Other horses are left behind after divorce. Many horses come from "ranch dispersal sales." They are working ranch-horses who are getting old and tired and can't really keep up with the younger horses anymore. They are frequently auctioned off, sometimes regardless of their health or disposition.

Finally, I've met a vast number of magnificent horses who have been rounded up and removed from open lands by the Bureau of Land Management (BLM) through systematic gathers designed to control horse populations. These horses end up going through the BLM's adoption program, where some are purchased into good homes. Sadly, many are not. And those

who spend three or four years in a holding facility, becoming too old to be trained, are often labeled unadoptable. There is nothing more depressing than a wild stallion who once ran freely across the vast plains and mountains of the West living out the remainder of his life in a crowded holding pen in the suburbs.

Wild horses have roamed the American West for centuries. It is estimated that there were once two million American wild horses in the West. This number is now estimated to be about twenty-seven thousand. The sad truth is that wild horses exist only for themselves and do not generate income for the BLM. They're beautiful but not profitable, and they must compete with large cattle interests and encroaching oil and gas drilling. The American wild horse may soon be a fading memory, as the number of horses living in certain "herd management areas" falls well below the population threshold necessary for the herd to survive. This is not accidental

The horse is a cultural icon of the American West and also plays a powerful archetypal role in people's lives. As the American wild horse is slowly and systematically being removed from public lands to make way for more hamburgers and gasoline, it saddens me deeply. I don't want to see us become like a virus, consuming and consuming until we literally die in our own waste.

THE BRIGHT SIDE OF LEARNING of the tragic fates of these horses was to discover the remarkable people who work to change them. Those who organize and run horse shelters and rescue organizations have a deep understanding of horses and devote their lives to reversing some very dysfunctional trends. Many of these facilities provide forgotten horses a life of dignity, one befitting the horses' innate design. Some horses find a permanent sanctuary there, a safe haven where they can live out the rest of their lives in peace and tranquility. They have room to roam, graze, and play — to be as nature intended horses to be. Thanks to these facilities, other horses find loving and supportive homes, where they live out the remainder of their lives as friends, companions, teachers, and healers.

Probably the most amazing and touching thing I observed at these facilities — I photographed at twenty, although there are hundreds throughout the country — is the love, compassion, and unconditional acceptance the staff members bring to the horses. In their own way, these people are helping to show us a way back to the values we have forgotten or discounted. They have learned to value caregiving over competition. They have learned that an authentic and mutually respectful relationship is far more important than cosmetic appearance or more money. They are learning and teaching that the connection between human and animal can be just as deep and profound as the connection between humans, oftentimes more so.

Many of the organizations do not stop at rescuing and placing horses. They also put tremendous effort into training, education, and outreach. Some are directly involved with Equine Assisted Therapy programs, in which

wounded horses help to heal wounded people, forming deep relationships across the fence. Some sanctuaries are also devoted to the conservation and preservation of rare or endangered breeds of wild horses. One in particular, Return to Freedom, has been instrumental in creating the nation's first wild horse conservancy and land trust, where family herds are allowed to live without separation or segregation, under the protection of national law.

Another organization, Rolling Dog Ranch, has devoted itself to the care and rehabilitation of blind horses, considered to be the most unwanted and useless of them all. While photographing these horses, the depth of connection touched me to the core. A quote on Rolling Dog's website embodies the essence of most of the shelters I have visited: "Each and every one of the horses loves being alive. That's really the ultimate inspiration for us. Despite their disabilities, they want nothing more than a chance to enjoy life. And that's what they get to do here." Isn't that what we all want?

ULTIMATELY, CREATING THIS BOOK has been amazingly rewarding for me. Sharing the beauty of these forgotten horses has been a much more satisfying challenge than doing another horse book on flashy, expensive breeds. I hope it further validates the remarkable work of these sanctuary heroes. Many nights I would find myself in a hotel room somewhere, reviewing images through a veil of tears. Through the photos, I felt the outpouring of love and care between the horses and people, and it touched me deeply. Never before have I felt so aligned with my life's purpose, and never before have I felt so moved by what I have experienced. The horses in this book have literally offered themselves to me, as they have offered themselves to humanity for thousands of years, and I am honored by their trust.

Our refusal to treat these horses — and other animals — as living, breathing equals has isolated us from the larger organism that supports and sustains our very lives. Our *work*, as many shelters and rescue organizations are showing us, is to begin to see ourselves as integral and equal parts of a complex and interdependent system of life, as illustrated by Chief Seattle's timeless words: "We did not create the web of life, we are merely a strand in it. What we do to the web, we do to ourselves."

The horses in this book are my heroes. They are the unwanted horses — the discarded, rejected horses who nobody cared about or could see any value in.... They are crooked, lame, ordinary, old, blind, uncontrollable, disrespectful, or unattractive. Many of them are just plain *wild*, a dirty word in this modern culture. I see tremendous beauty in them, and I want to share that beauty.

My hope with this book is to help redirect our collective perception, to help redefine how we see beauty, and thereby help to restore balance to our world. May the horses in this book reveal their soul to you, as they have to me. May they show us a way back to a deep appreciation both of the world around us, and of each other.

Tony Stromberg,
January 2008

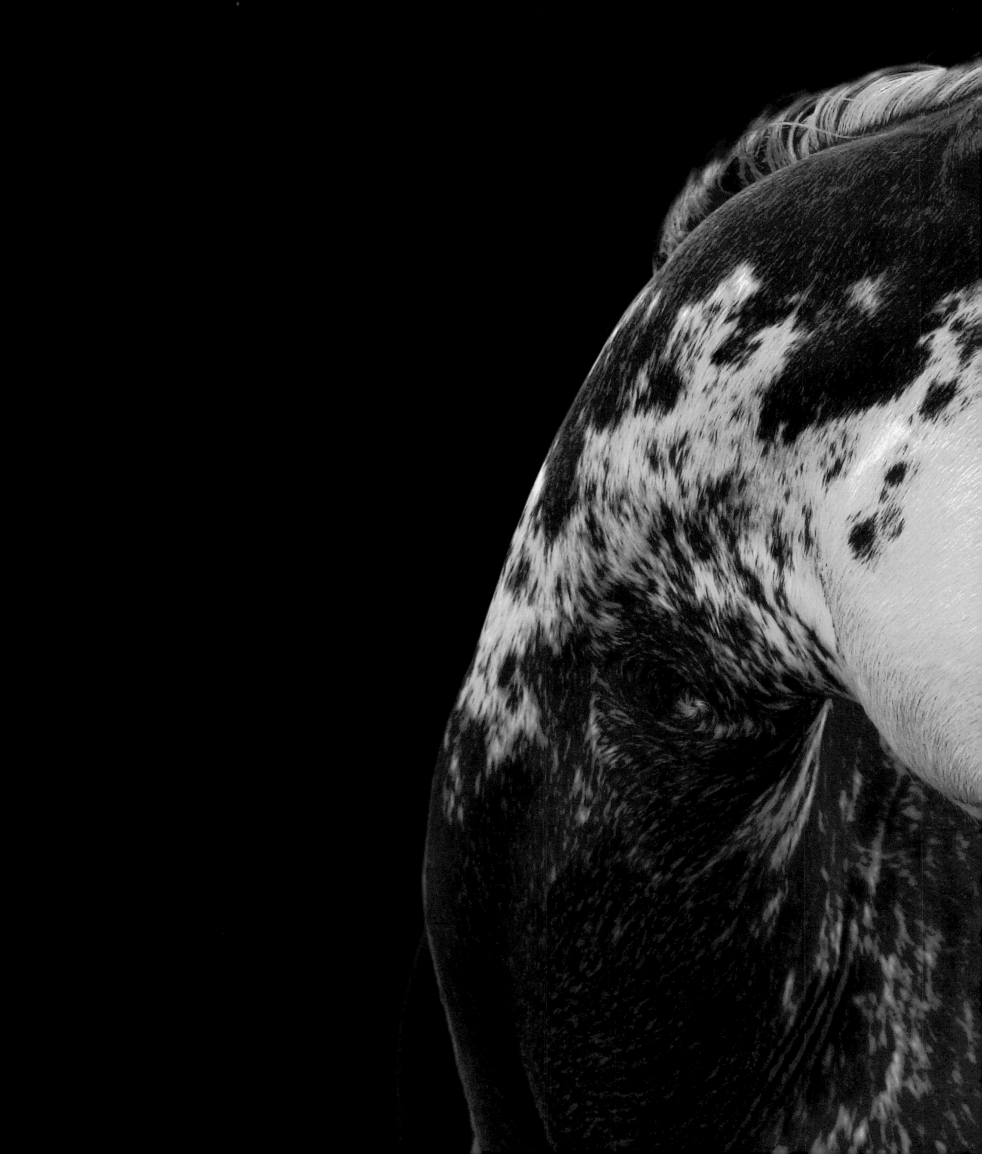

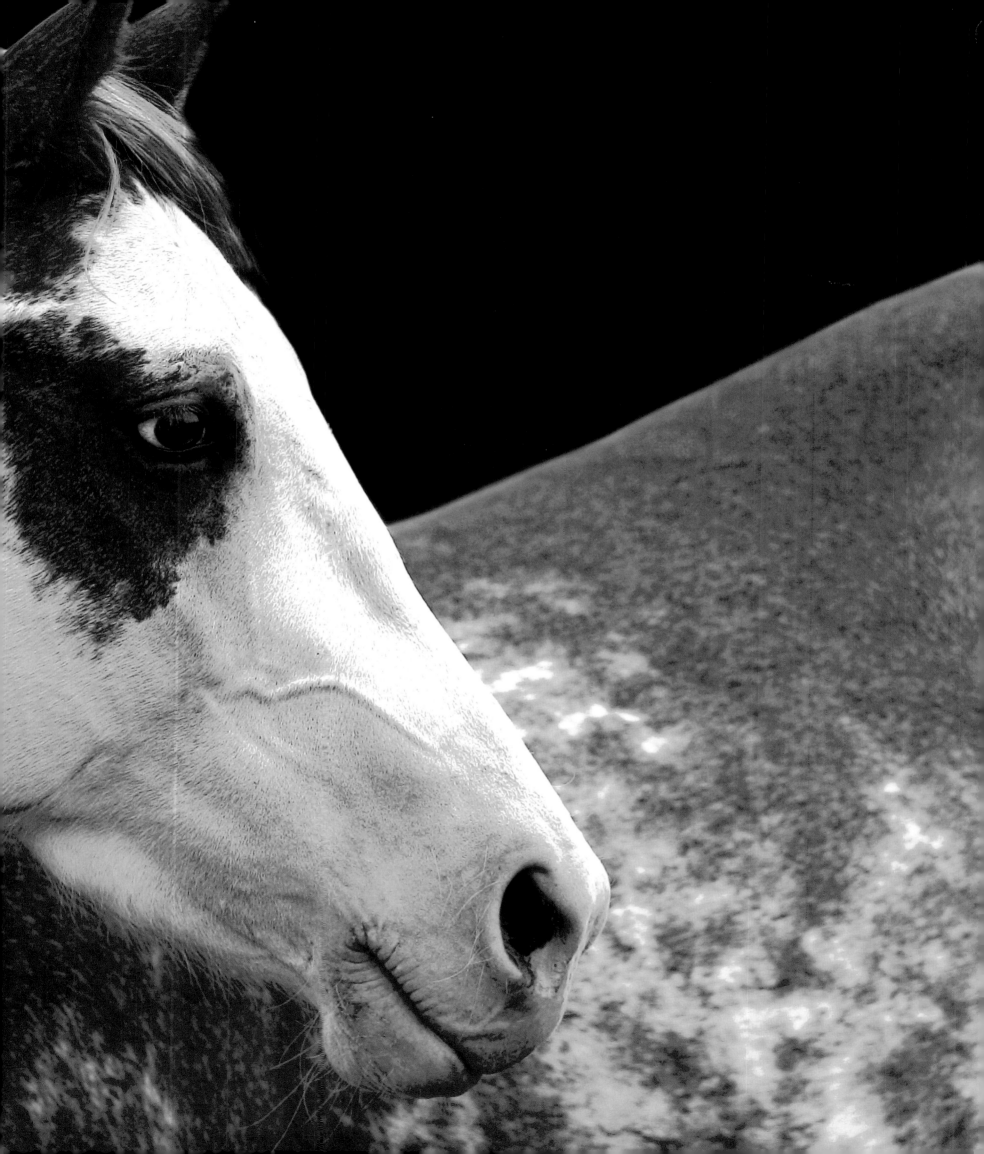

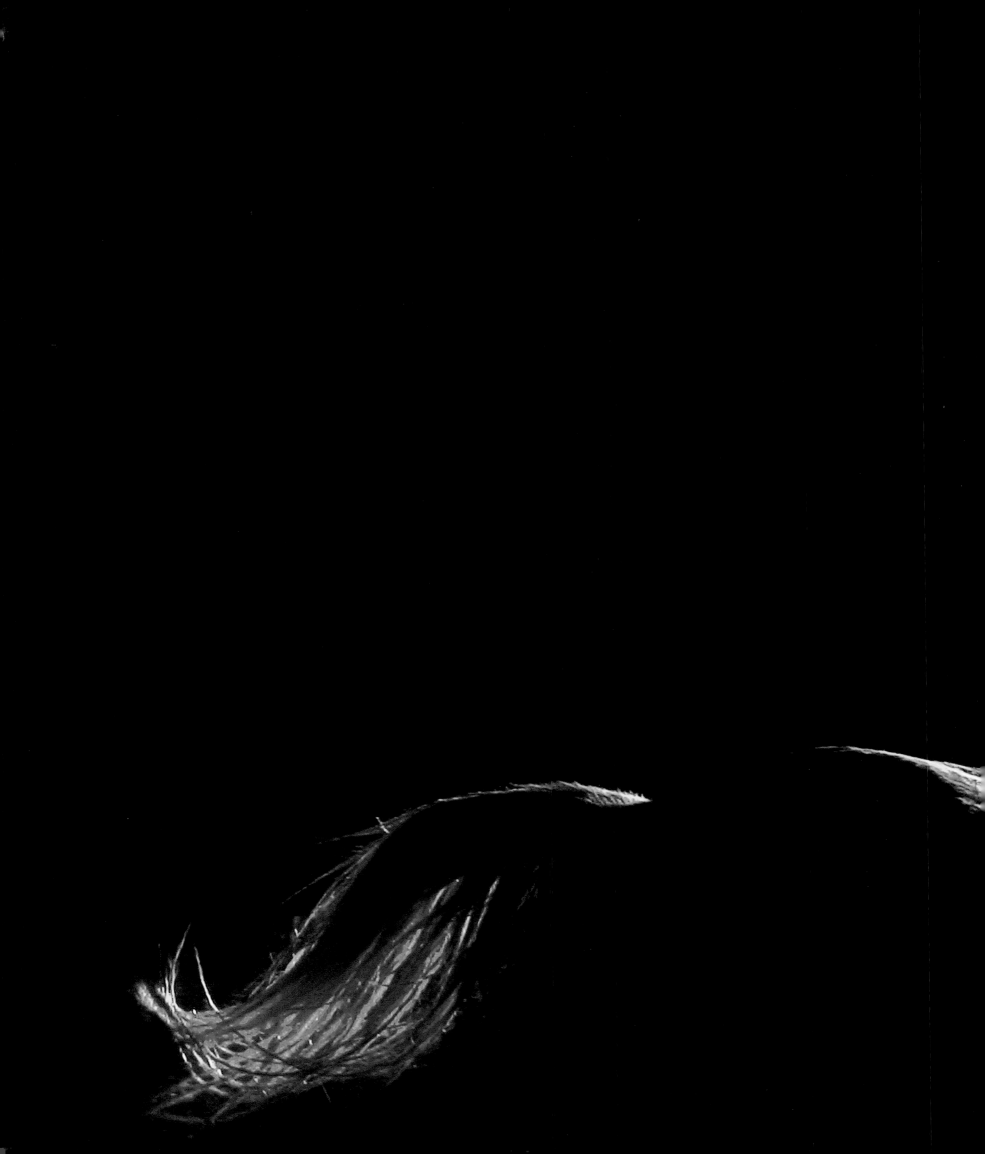

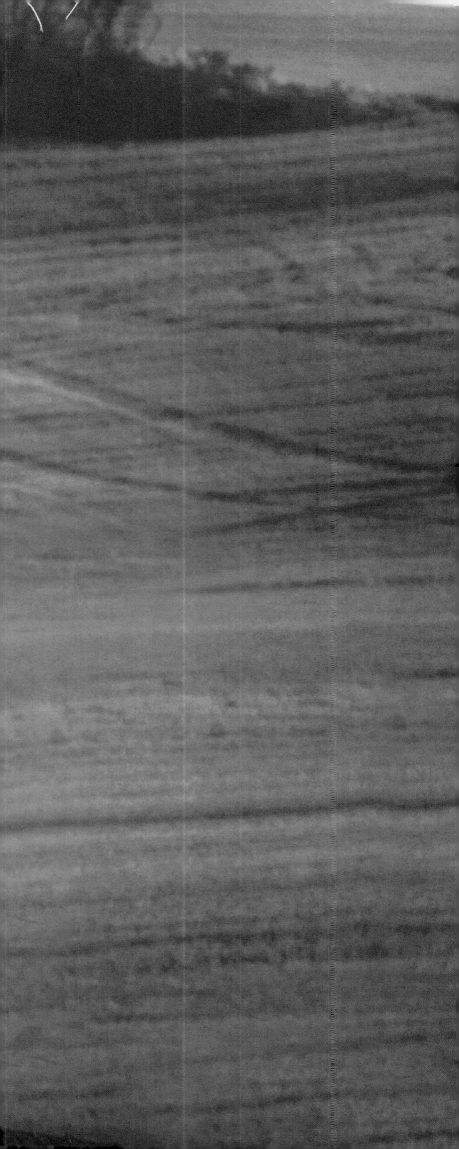

For more information about specific photographs, including where they were taken, please visit www.tonystromberg.com.

≈ BLACK HILLS WILD HORSE SANCTUARY

Dayton Hyde and Susan Watt
P.O. Box 998
Hot Springs, SD 57747
(800) 252-6652
www.wildmustangs.com

The Black Hills Wild Horse Sanctuary, founded by Dayton O. Hyde, is about helping any wild horse in need. Over five hundred wild horses (including American Spanish, Sulphur, and Kiger mustangs as well as herds from state governments, Bureau of Land Management land, and Forest Service land) make their home on eleven thousand acres in the pristine Black Hills of South Dakota. The wild horse herds graze on prairie grasses and water in the Cheyenne River, which winds through wild canyonlands in the heart of the sanctuary.

≈ THE EPONA PROJECT

Kellie Gibbs and Susan Ramsey
2004 Lake Gulch Road
Castle Rock, CO 80104
(303) 814-0085
www.hometown.aol.com/theeponaproject/epona-home.html

The Epona Project is a Colorado nonprofit that uses cutting-edge natural horsemanship techniques and traditional horse training methods to rescue, rehabilitate, gentle, and train wild and problem horses. The project also provides education for the horses' owners and for other horse enthusiasts. The Epona Project was created to help the many horses that are abandoned, neglected, mishandled, mistreated, sent to slaughter auctions, or improperly trained and that can benefit from a very specialized rehabilitative approach.

≈ EQUINE ADVOCATES

Susan Wagner
P.O. Box 354
Chatham, NY 12037
(518) 245-1599
www.equineadvocates.com

Equine Advocates uses education, investigation, rescue operations, and public outreach in order to rescue and protect horses and to prevent their abuse. The organization deals primarily with five important issues: equine rescue, the abolition of horse slaughter, wild horse protection, the abolition of the PMU (pregnant mares' urine) industry, and the prevention of equine abuse.

≈ THE HORSE SHELTER

100 AB Old Cash Ranch Road
Cerrilllos, NM 87010
(505) 471-6179
www.thehorseshelter.org

The Horse Shelter is a nonprofit organization dedicated to the rescue of abused and neglected horses within the state of New Mexico. The staff of the Horse Shelter is dedicated to providing a safe, healthy, and loving environment for rescued horses. They follow up on every report of horse abuse or neglect they receive. In addition, they provide information on proper horse care for horse owners and make every attempt to assist individuals with the care of their horses. They pursue legal action in abuse cases when necessary.

≈ INTERNATIONAL SOCIETY FOR THE PROTECTION OF MUSTANGS AND BURROS

Karen Sussman
P.O. Box 55
Lantry, SD 57636
(605) 964-6866
www.ispmb.org

Located on the Cheyenne River Sioux Indian Reservation in South Dakota, the International Society for the Protection of Mustang and Burros (ISPMB) is an empowering force, influencing global attitudes and catalyzing actions for the protection, preservation, and understanding of wild horses and burros and their habitat. Situated on 680 acres, the ISPMB cares for three separate and unique wild horse herds. As the first wild horse and burro organization in the United States, the ISPMB provided sophisticated advocacy programs and public forums and received the support of Congress.

≈ LASTING PARTNERSHIP TRAINING CENTER, INC.

Michelle Conner
25175 East Highway 110
Calhan, CO 80808
(719) 651-3662
www.lastingpartnership.com

Lasting Partnership Training Center (LPTC) is a training and boarding center located east of Colorado Springs. LPTC is dedicated to creating lasting partnerships between horses and humans using natural horsemanship methods. Its staff members ensure that the horses are provided with the best care possible and that the horses' human partners are given the knowledge they need to create and maintain healthy, happy, lasting partnerships with their equine friends.

≈ THE MUSTANG CENTER, LLC

Diane Kennedy
10433 Dillon Road
Louisville, CO 80027
(720) 940-8873
www.themustangcenter.com

The Mustang Center is an education, outreach, and adoption facility located along Colorado's Front Range that promotes awareness, appreciation, and adoption of mustangs. Using natural horsemanship approaches, the center fosters, gentles, and trains mustangs removed from Bureau of Land Management (BLM) properties. In accordance with BLM requirements, the center's horses are available for adoption or purchase. Visitors to the center can meet mustangs, learn about their history and legacy, and discover ways to help preserve this unique emblem of the American West. The center also offers educational programs and counseling for those who are considering adopting or who have adopted a mustang.

≈ THE NEW MEXICAN WILD HORSE PROJECT

Campbell Ranch Preserve
P.O. Box 681
Socorro, NM 87801
www.nmhp.org

The New Mexican Wild Horse Project brings together key individuals who love wild horses for the purpose of promoting healthy herds, enhancing and protecting their habitat, and encouraging community involvement. The project is concerned only with the preservation and protection of the breed. The horses that live in the project's preserves will never be sold.

≈ ORPHAN ACRES

Brent Glover
1183 Rothfork Road
Viola, ID 83872
(208) 882-9293
http://community.palouse.net/orphanacres

The mission of Orphan Acres Equine Rescue, Rehabilitation, and Sanctuary is to provide care and rehabilitation for abandoned, neglected, abused, and malnourished horses and to educate the public about the issues surrounding rescue, rehabilitation, and all aspects of horse ownership and care. Since its inception, Orphan Acres has found homes for over 1,450 animals. Animals that are too old or have too many problems to be safely adopted become members of the Orphan Acres permanent herd.

≈ REDWINGS HORSE SANCTUARY

47240 Lockwood-Jolon Road
Lockwood, CA 93932
(831) 386-0135
www.redwings.org

The mission of Redwings Horse Sanctuary is to rescue abused and neglected equines, provide permanent sanctuary or foster homes for those equines, and eliminate the causes of equine suffering through education and community outreach programs. Redwings has initiated several programs to address educational, financial, and other factors behind equine neglect, including an equine education program for new owners and an equine medical assistance program for owners with low incomes.

≈ REFUGE FARMS, INC.

Sandra Gilbert
P.O. Box 195
Spring Valley, WI 54767
(715) 772-3379
www.refugefarms.org

Since 2002, a total of forty-one horses have come to Refuge Farms for sanctuary. Each horse is given humane treatment, plenty of food and water, and a permanent home on the farm. Besides offering these benefits, Refuge Farms is developing a program called Horses Helping, in which human beings experience deep emotional healing as a result of sharing time with the horses. The horses provide empathetic, nonjudgmental listening that helps troubled people heal and regain self-acceptance. Recovery can occur for both humans and horses, in tiny steps, when they interact without judgment or criticism from each other — with only unconditional love.

≈ RETURN TO FREEDOM AMERICAN WILD HORSE SANCTUARY

Neda DeMayo
P.O. Box 926
Lompoc, CA 93438
(805) 737-9246
www.returntofreedom.org

Return to Freedom provides a safe haven for herds of wild horses and burros that might otherwise be divided, slaughtered, abused, or left to roam without food or water. The sanctuary allows these animals to live out their lives in freedom while simultaneously creating an opportunity for people to directly experience part of America's living heritage — the wild horse in its natural habitat. By adopting entire herds, Return to Freedom maintains intact family and social bands so that wild horses can continue to live in natural herd groups according to their geographic origins. Return to Freedom is working to expand its model into a larger scale wild horse conservancy — a historical land trust — where threatened strains of wild horses can continue to live in herds.

≈ ROCKY MOUNTAIN FOAL RESCUE
(Closed in early 2008)

Established in 2000, Rocky Mountain Foal Rescue closed in early 2008 due to an injury suffered by the founder. In the seven years it was active, RMFR placed over four hundred rescued horses into loving homes.

≈ ROLLING DOG RANCH ANIMAL SANCTUARY

Steve Smith and Alayne Marker
400 Rolling Dog Ranch Lane
Ovando, MT 59854
(406) 793-6000
www.rollingdogranch.org

Steve Smith and Alayne Marker founded the Rolling Dog Ranch Animal Sanctuary in December 2000, shortly after moving to the ranch permanently. When they bought the property in the summer of 1998, their dream was to turn the 160 acres of open grassland and cottonwoods into a sanctuary for disabled animals — the animals least likely to be adopted and most likely to be euthanized in traditional shelters. The ranch is now home to nearly eighty animals, more than half of them blind.

≈ RUBY RANCH HORSE RESCUE

Pat Miller and Roger Kavan
36785 Ramah Road E.
Ramah, CO 80832
(719) 541-3642
www.rrhr.net

Ruby Ranch Horse Rescue (RRHR) is a nonprofit organization dedicated to providing shelter, care, and rehabilitation for abused, neglected, abandoned, and unwanted horses, including horses that can no longer be cared for by their owners and horses at risk of going to slaughter. RRHR strives to place each horse into a permanent, caring, and positive environment that will be mutually beneficial to both horse and human.

≈ TRANQUILITY FARM

Priscilla Clark
P.O. Box 210
Tehachapi, CA 93581
(661) 823-0307
www.tranquilityfarmtbs.org

Tranquility Farm accepts the donation of thoroughbred horses from racetracks and breeding farms, with the goal of giving each horse the best opportunity to find an adoptive home. For those horses that are not readily adoptable, the farm offers comfortable retirement whenever possible, giving priority to horses that have been significant competitors or producers. Tranquility Farm requests but does not require that owners contribute sponsorship to help defray the costs of rehabilitation and retraining. No horse is denied acceptance into Tranquility Farm based on the owner's financial contribution.

≈ TWIN WILLOWS RANCH

P.O. Box 199
Ocate, NM 87734
(505) 666-2028
www.twinwillowsranch.com

Twin Willows Ranch is an idyllic family ranch located on over 2,200 private and secluded acres in rural northern New Mexico. Previously a recognized performance horse operation, the ranch has evolved to become a sanctuary for animals seeking a life of dignity, respect, and the finest care. The ranch is currently the home of Tony Stromberg and his wife, Claudia, who act as its resident caretakers and managers.

≈ WALKIN' N CIRCLES RANCH, INC.

P.O. Box 626
Edgewood, NM 87015
(505) 286-0779
www.wncr.org

The Walkin' N Circles Ranch (WNCR) provides a safe, comfortable home for horses that have been neglected or abused or that are no longer wanted by their owners. WNCR's founders and volunteers believe in the humane treatment of animals. At the ranch, horses receive food, grooming, medical treatments, rehabilitation, emotional care, safe shelter, daily care, and the chance to live a dignified life. The staff strives to rehabilitate and retrain equines for adoption into special, well-screened homes where they can again serve a useful purpose, be loved by others, and reclaim their self-esteem.